G000025622

# CONTENTS

# FOREWORD

It was a day, just like any other day. There was no 'inner voice' of warning, no heaviness of spirit - it was an ordinary day. My son and his wife had brought their new baby son to visit me, and as we laughed and chatted together, I played with my grandson, 'walking' him up my chest and down again when suddenly his little foot struck what felt like a stone in my breast. The smile stayed on my face, but a chill gripped my heart and as soon as my family left I hurried to the bathroom to examine myself, and my fears were confirmed – there was a large, craggy, painless lump in my breast, and it felt as if the sun had gone behind the clouds, and I entered that 'valley of deep shadow'.

Here was I, a christian minister's wife, a counsellor and comforter of others, happy and fulfilled in my life in every way, and suddenly the sun had ceased to shine – I had no doubt what this lump was, even then. Later, after I had shared the news with my husband, the doctor confirmed my thoughts and after various tests the lump was shown to be a cancerous tumour.

My relationship with God for many years had been a blessed one in every way, in spite of different bereavements and trials common to most people, but now I faced a dilemma that brought a deep inner struggle: could I still trust him, when I didn't understand what he was doing in my life? The questioning intensified when, a year later, the cancer re-occurred and I needed more surgery and treatment. It is now over two years after the onset of the illness and I still don't fully understand, but I have learned that meaningful prayer and worship is to put myself more into God's hands and to trust him, and in doing so to experience a certain joy and peace that comes from living 'Just for today'.

All my devotional poems have come from my personal christian experience, special times when the Lord has spoken to me about something specifically, and I seek to portray in my paintings something of the beauty of God's creation. My hope is that this book can in some way be a blessing and a help to others to draw nearer to God through his son, Jesus, and especially for those who live 'Just for today'. May you also find, as I have done, that the Lord is with you even in the valley of deep shadow.

B. Kaye Jones

*My mouth shall show forth thy righteousness
and thy salvation all the day;
for I know not the numbers thereof.*

PSALM 71:15

# JUST FOR TODAY, LORD

Just for today, Lord, O help me live just for today.
I'm realizing that I can live no other way.
Grace for today, Lord, is all I need and all I ask;
tomorrow's trials are hid from view –
I'm glad it's so –
the future I don't want to know;
it's in your hands and I can rest and leave it there –
safely within your care.

Just for today, Lord, O help me live just for today,
my greatest longing, that I will trust you and obey.
Faith for today, Lord, is all I need and all I ask;
to fill your footsteps, and follow as you go before,
each day to trust a little more,
to take the path that you have purposed just for me –
faith doesn't need to see.

Just for today, Lord, O help me live just for today,
found leaning on you, if skies are blue or dismal grey.
Strength for today, Lord, is all I need and all I ask;
to cheer the weary, to smile and say 'I understand,
we need to hold the Saviour's hand,
his strength is mighty for the weak and for the sad –
making the weary glad.'

# THE SHEEP

We've roamed the downs for many a mile –
we know each hedge, and fence, and stile –
and rested by the pond awhile,
but now we're coming home.

Our Shepherd knows us all by name;
to him, no two are quite the same.
He tends the sick, and helps the lame
to make the journey home.

Our Shepherd knows just where to lead,
and understands our want and need;
in pastures green he lets us feed,
upon the journey home.

At last, at night, safe in the fold,
away from danger, fear and cold;
no cunning fox, though he be bold,
can spoil our rest at home.

*Lord Jesus, that great Shepherd of the sheep.*

HEBREWS 13:20

# OLD-FASHIONED FLOWERS

Old-fashioned flowers, in old English gardens:
hollyhocks scarlet, lavender blue;
pansies of velvet and sweet-smelling roses;
purple delphiniums, irises, too.


Old-fashioned flowers, like old-fashioned virtues:
gentleness, purity, goodness and grace
give to the life an enhancement of beauty –
speech full of charity, softness of face.


*. . . and let the beauty of the Lord our God*
*be upon us . . .*

PSALM 90:17

# THE VALLEY OF
# DEEP SHADOW

In the Valley of the Shadow
there are mists that bring confusion,
there are shocks that disillusion,
there are dangers, causing fear:
in the Valley of the Shadow
there's no sun to light the pathway,
and you hear the tempter's voice say,
'Your Good Shepherd isn't here.'

As you travel through the valley
and it seems you've lost direction,
needing comfort and affection,
feel the Shepherd doesn't care;
you can find him in the valley
if, by faith, you reach and touch him,
though the mists of doubt the path dim,
for the Shepherd's always there.

He will take you through the valley,
with his love his sheep protecting,
and your hidden path directing,
to that city, bright and fair.
Claim his promise in the valley,
rise above the doubt and fearing,
see the light of Heaven appearing;
night has gone; there's no death there.

*Yea, though I walk through*
*the valley of the shadow of death,*
*I will fear no evil: for thou art with me;*
*thy rod and thy staff they comfort me.*

PSALM 23:4

13

# BRIDGES

If I can be a bridge between
an alien world and you;
If I can be a bridge between
two folks of different view;

If I can be a bridge between
the old ways and the new:
then I fulfil the law of love
in everything I do.


*Blessed are the peacemakers;*
*for they shall be called the children of God.*

MATTHEW 5:9

# ANGEL UNAWARE

That Jesus loves the little ones
is very plain to see,
and when he lived on earth,
the children sat upon his knee.
'Safe in the arms of Jesus'
is a saying we all know,
and for the dear ones given to him,
we really know it's so.

We had a precious little one,
a candle flickering dim,
who lived and taught us many things,
and then went home to him,
who taught us that God's ways are best,
and that his grace is there,
in trials and tests we find him close,
and feel his loving care.

One day, all things shall be revealed,
we'll understand his plan,
But while we live on earth,
we'll trust, as bravely as we can
that he knows best his little ones,
and how they touch each heart –
a softening comes; a work of grace is done;
and then we part.

*And Jesus called a little child unto him.*

MATTHEW 18:2

*The Kingdom of God is not meat and drink;*
*but righteousness and peace*
*and joy in the Holy Ghost.*

ROMANS 14:17

# LOVE, JOY AND PEACE

O God of joy, we worship and adore thee –
we see thy hand, in every perfect thing;
each tiny flower, each sunset and each rainbow,
in rolling sea, and bird upon the wing,
who makes our hearts to thrill at thy creation,
great God of joy, our praise to thee we bring.


O God of love, you sent your son to suffer,
to bleed and die, to save our souls from sin,
your heart was grieved to see creation fallen,
till Jesus came, each erring one to win;
to bring us back, from darkness and from bondage,
great God of love, give us thy love within.


O God of peace, our hearts are still before thee,
our struggles cease, when only thee we see.
O let thy peace now comfort and surround us,
and fill our hearts, and set our spirits free
from strife and hate,
from stress and inward pressure,
great God of peace, that we may worship thee.

# Do you have a dream?

Do you have a dream –
of a cottage, in the country,
with a garden and a stream:
soft, white doves nestling
in a roof of thatch –
and 'canine greetings'
as you lift the latch?

Yes, I had a dream –
roses in profusion, rambling,
round my home that might-have-been.
But there's no grieving for
what cannot be –
my Father has
prepared a place for me!

*In my Father's house are many mansions . . .*
*I go to prepare a place for you.*

JOHN 14:2

*A new heart also will I give you,*
*and a new spirit will I put within you:*
*and I will take away the stony heart out of your flesh,*
*and I will give you a heart of flesh.*

EZEKIEL 36:26

# THE SOFT HEART

I long to know you more, dear Lord,
I long to seek your face;
take out the hardness, Lord, and put
your softness in its place.

I long to have a soft heart, Lord,
a heart that's open wide
for your pure love, a heart that knows
your Spirit, deep inside.

I long to see with your eyes, Lord,
to view things from above;
not as the world would view a soul,
but give me eyes of love.

I long to have a mind like yours,
a mind that's clear and free,
a mind renewed, refreshed, revived,
that Heaven I may see.

# O THAT I HAD WINGS
## LIKE A DOVE

There have been times when
I felt I grasped your mind
through the dim uncertainties
of things I felt I knew;
In part I saw your Great Plan, and your design,
then mists of doubt obscured that better view.

O that my spirit, like a soaring bird of song,
through the sparkling morning air,
bent on some heavenly quest,
could rise above the poor efforts of my prayers,
and Heaven reached, come winging home to rest.

O Holy Spirit, like a gentle dove of peace,
softly wing your way to rest here,
in my waiting heart
enveloping all I have and all I am –
your presence in my life in every part.

*Oh, that I had wings like a dove!*
*For then would I fly away,*
*and be at rest.*

PSALM 55:6

# STILL LIFE

In these days of seeming uselessness,
Lord, give me grace:
to keep a cheerful spirit,
a smile upon my face.
In these days of inactivity,
O Lord, I ask –
as others hurry by me,
bent on some useful task –
don't let me feel a servant
of some poor, useless estate;
remind me that they also serve
who only stand and wait.


*O Lord, truly I am thy servant.*

PSALM 116:16

# OUR GOOD SHEPHERD

I want to tell you, that in spite of what you feel
God's love is real:
that in spite of what you are,
he's never far away
and in time of doubt and fear
he's always near.
So just turn around, and take his hand, and pray.

But now you tell me that you feel too dark to pray,
you've turned away:
it is night-time in your heart,
in every part of you.
I really know just how you feel,
but he can heal
if you do the thing he's telling you to do.

The Bible tells us, when our hearts are hard and cold
outside the fold,
the Good Shepherd seeks the lost –
at greatest cost and pain.
His great love will seek us out
so never doubt:
he will find his lamb, and lead him home again.

*'I am the Good Shepherd, and know my sheep . . . .'*

John 10:14

*Let us run with patience the race
that is set before us, looking unto Jesus.*

HEBREWS 12:1-2

# Anniversary

Before we walk another mile,
we climb a hill, and pause awhile,
to view the path our feet have trod,
a path that has been planned by God.
We see behind us youth's bright love;
enthusiasm; while above
the Lord has watched the rolling years
of struggles, heartbreaks, laughs and tears
– experiences we have shared,
and faith-steps, tremblingly dared
– by this maturity is gained
and deepening love to God, unfeigned,
a richer fellowship we share,
and greater is our love and care,
as in each other we see him
– his brightness that will not grow dim.
So courage, dear heart, in the race,
and new hope, as we turn and face
the pathway to our future years
– for brighter, brighter light appears
to show us where to place our feet,
as on the road we run to meet
Christ Jesus, Saviour of our souls,
for in his hands our lives he holds.

# GARDENS

Joy can be found in a garden –
walk and talk,
stop and look,
sit and dream.
Never be rushed through a garden –
look with care,
everywhere
jewels gleam.

*And the Lord God planted a garden eastward
in Eden; and there he put the man whom
he had formed.*

GENESIS 2:8

# My Friend

Jesus my Lord, Fairest of Ten Thousand,
star of my night, thy brightness shows the way,
Jesus my Lord, O come beloved Saviour,
quicken my heart, to worship as I pray.

Jesus my Lord, loved me ere I knew him.
When I was lost, and wandering far away,
Jesus my Lord, loving Shepherd, found me,
safe in his arms, he brought me home to stay.

Jesus my Lord, precious Friend forever,
guiding my life, I feel his presence near,
Jesus my Lord, gentle Saviour, draws me
close to his side, his loving voice to hear.

*. . . there is a friend that sticketh closer
than a brother.*

PROVERBS 18:24

# The Fruitful Life

Dear Lord, for these four things I ask:

A mind that's full of wisdom
a heart that's full of love,
a spirit full of faith and hope,
a joy from Heaven above.

*But the fruit of the Spirit is love, joy, peace . . .*

GALATIANS 5:22

35

# SEE THE KING

(part 1 – Christmas)

See the King – born in stable mean and poor.
See the King – lies upon his bed of straw.
See the King of Heaven to earth come down.
See the King, upon his head no crown.

See the King – lowly ox and ass stand by.
See the King – in the sky a star on high
shows to those who seek – a King is born,
tiny child, in stable all forlorn.
He's the King.

See the King – by the word of God foretold.
See the King – prophesied from days of old
that one day – Emmanuel would come,
Prince of Peace, Messiah, God's own Son.

See the King – there's no sceptre in his hand.
See the King – born unknown in Eastern land.
Let us come like shepherds to adore,
bring our praise, and bend the knee before
Christ the King.

'Where is he that is born King of the Jews?'

MATTHEW 2:2

*. . . and (Pilate) saith unto the Jews,
Behold your King!*

John 19:14

# SEE THE KING

## (part 2 – Easter)

See the King – by the word of God foretold.
See the King – prophesied from days of old
that one day Emmanuel would come,
Prince of Peace, Messiah, God's own Son.

See the King – man of sorrows and of pain.
See the King – men revile that holy Name.
See the King of Heaven to earth come down.
See the King – upon his head a crown;
crown of thorns.

See the King – jeering soldiers standing by.
See the King – Heav'n weeps with darkened sky.
See the King – rejected, crucified.
See the King for sinful man has died.

See the King – seated now at God's right hand.
See the King – glorified in Heaven's land.
Let us come with angels to adore,
bring our praise, and bow the knee before
Christ the King.

# Man of Sorrows

O Man of Sorrows, the world would despise you,
denying your glory, disdaining your cross;
unable to grasp at the life you would offer,
and thus disregarding your suffering and loss.

O gentle Healer, the poor and the needy
were served by the hands later nailed to the tree.
You reached out and touched them,
and moved by your mercy,
they reached out to touch you,
and found they were free.

O lowly Servant, despised and rejected,
they misunderstood you, desiring a King
with pomp and with splendour, to rule over nations,
not seeing your kingdom was hidden within.

O Lamb of God, as a sheep to the slaughter,
they led you to die, for our sorrow and sin.
The ultimate sacrifice, blood of atonement
was shed for our guilt, our redemption to win.

Conquering Saviour, in death you have triumphed
by breaking the curse and the power of the grave.
Now risen, victorious, King of all glory,
almighty to conquer, almighty to save.

*He is despised and rejected of men; a man of sorrows
and acquainted with grief ... Surely he hath borne
our griefs, and carried our sorrows ...*

ISAIAH 53:3,4

41

# Our English Sunday

O, may there always be
a 'Sabbath rest by Galilee',
a calm and quiet day, when we
stop, and replenish energy.

O, may there always be
that 'silence of eternity',
the peace of christianity –
Sunday's sweet tranquillity.

*. . . come . . . and rest a while . . .*

MARK 6:31

*Well done, thou good and faithful servant . . .*
*enter thou into the joy of thy Lord.*

MATTHEW 25:21

# THE SHEEP DOGS

The master calls, and we obey,
we'll listen to each word he'll say,
and never do the work *our* way
to bring the sheep-flock home.

We must be vigilant, and true,
and diligent in all we do,
to help him bring the sheep right through
the dangers, going home.

And if we see some sheep adrift
we follow them, with feet so swift
and bring them back, so there's no rift
in our flock, coming home.

Now we're content, our job well done;
the yearly shearing has begun
and we can rest, as sinks the sun;
we've made the journey home.

# HEALING

I felt your healing touch, the other day –
not in my body, but in my soul;
the hurts and needs and fears all disappeared –
your healing touch had made me free and whole.

I felt your healing touch, the other day –
in both my spirit, and in my soul;
a joy, and faith and love rose in my heart –
your healing touch had made my spirit whole.

I need your healing touch, this very day –
here in my body, not in my soul;
I ask according to your precious word –
your healing touch will make me fully whole.


*Heal me, O Lord, and I shall be healed . . .*

JEREMIAH 17:14

*I am the Lord that healeth thee.*

EXODUS 15:26

# Just for Today

## Devotional Poems

Written and illustrated
by
B. Kaye Jones

Kevin
Mayhew

First published in Great Britain in 1993 by
KEVIN MAYHEW LTD
Rattlesden
Bury St Edmunds
Suffolk IP30 0SZ


ISBN 0 86209 465 8

© 1993 Kevin Mayhew Limited

Printed in Hong Kong
by Colorcraft